Service
&
Mentoring

Look for these topics in the
Everyday Matters Bible Studies for Women

Acceptance	Mentoring
Bible Study & Meditation	Outreach
Celebration	Prayer
Community	Reconciliation
Confession	Sabbath Rest
Contemplation	Service
Faith	Silence
Fasting	Simplicity
Forgiveness	Solitude
Gratitude	Stewardship
Hospitality	Submission
Justice	Worship

Service
&
Mentoring

Spiritual Practices
FOR EVERYDAY LIFE

**Everyday Matters Bible Studies for Women—
Service & Mentoring**

Printed in the United States of America

First Printing — January 2015

Contents

Everyday Matters Bible Studies for Women

Mentoring

Holy Habits

Spiritual Practices for Everyday Life

Everyday life today is busier and more distracting than it has ever been before. While cell phones and texting make it easier to keep track of children and each other, they also make it harder to get away from the demands that overwhelm us. Time, it seems, is a shrinking commodity. But God, the Creator of time, has given us the keys to leading a life that may be challenging but not overwhelming. In fact, he offers us tools to do what seems impossible and come away refreshed and renewed. These tools are called spiritual practices, or spiritual disciplines.

Spiritual practices are holy habits. They are rooted in God's word, and they go back to creation itself. God has hard-wired us to thrive when we obey him, even when it seems like his instructions defy our "common sense." When we engage in the holy habits that God has ordained, time takes on a new dimension. What seems impossible is actually easy; it's easy because we are tapping into God's resources.

The holy habits that we call spiritual practices are all geared to position us in a place where we can allow the Holy Spirit to work in us and through us, to grant us power and strength to do the things we can't do on our own. They take us to a place where we can become intimate with God.

While holy habits and everyday life may sound like opposites, they really aren't.

As you learn to incorporate spiritual practices into your life, you'll find that everyday life is easier. At the same time, you will draw closer to God and come to a place where you can luxuriate in his rich blessings. Here is a simple example. Elizabeth Collings hated running household errands. Picking up dry cleaning, doing the grocery shopping, and chauffeuring her kids felt like a never-ending litany of menial chores. One day she had a simple realization that changed her life. That day she began to use her "chore time" as a time of prayer and fellowship with God.

Whenever Elizabeth walked the aisle of the supermarket, she prayed for each person who would eat the item of food she selected. On her way to pick up her children, she would lay their lives out before God, asking him to be there for them even when she couldn't. Each errand became an opportunity for fellowship with God. The chore that had been so tedious became a precious part of her routine that she cherished.

The purpose of these study guides is to help you use spiritual practices to make your own life richer, fuller, and deeper. The series includes twenty-four spiritual practices that are the building blocks of Christian spiritual formation. Each practice is a holy habit that has been modeled for us in the Bible. The practices are acceptance, Bible study and meditation, celebration, community, confession, contemplation, faith, fasting, forgiveness, gratitude, hospitality, justice, mentoring, outreach, prayer, reconciliation, Sabbath rest, service, silence, simplicity, solitude, stewardship, submission, and worship.

As you move through the practices that you select, remember Christ's promise in Matthew 11:28–30:

> *Come to me, all of you who are weary and carry heavy burdens. Take my yoke upon you. Let me teach you, because I am humble and gentle at heart, and you will find rest for your souls. For my yoke is easy to bear, and the burden I give you is light.*

Introduction

to the Practice of Service & Mentoring

One of the principal rules of religion is to lose no occasion of serving God. And, since he is invisible to our eyes, we are to serve him in our neighbor; which he receives as if done to himself in person, standing visibly before us.

—John Wesley

For those us of who are "doers" and more comfortable with "visible spiritual disciplines," considering the disciplines of service and mentoring can bring a sense of relief and delight. Finally, action verbs! Something to *do*! And certainly both of these spiritual practices will most likely have results that are easier to identify than some of the less tangible practices. It's easy to think we'll grapple less with understanding these disciplines than ones such as fasting or confession. In some ways, that's probably true. Service takes many forms, and we're familiar with it from an early age.

While service as a spiritual discipline has much in common with service in general, it is also very different; the lessons that follow will show how and why. Their purpose is to help you break through any obstacles that may be daunting and to understand why Jesus so emphasized service.

While service may well be a practice to which all believers are called, the practice of mentoring is another story. Defined as "an experienced and trusted adviser," a mentor is usually older than the person being mentored and has gained a greater degree of knowledge, wisdom, and experience in a particular area over a period of years. But as Mindy Caliguire says in her article "Why We Mentor" (*Everyday Matters Bible for Women*), the most important qualities for a mentor are love and genuine concern for another individual. "As a mentor," she says, "you can actually care about someone's spiritual development and are willing to come alongside her for a season of her journey."

Both service and mentoring give us the opportunity to learn and to teach. Our goal will be to reacquaint ourselves with both serving and mentoring, for God desires us to be ever on a continuum of learning and teaching, of serving and being served. Such a rhythm keeps us sane, refreshed, inventive, and humble.

As you go about these visible disciplines of service and mentoring, offer yourself for tasks to be done—and be aware that God, as usual, is up to something we cannot see. Yes, there are needs, and you are part of the solution. And yet God has something for you as well within the service and within the mentoring. He has plans to use it to grow *you* in discipleship.

Service

CHAPTER 1

Whom Shall We Serve?

The Good Samaritan Example

"Then a despised Samaritan came along, and when
he saw the man, he felt compassion for him."

LUKE 10:33

For this study, read Luke 10:25–37.

Years ago, I worked at an organization with wonderful
people who were eager to serve the Lord. One day a co-
worker came in distressed. In an effort to not go into debt,
the family was using the local laundromat while saving up
to pay cash for a new washer. The night before, the family
left the laundromat briefly, and returned to find that someone had stolen all their clothes out of the machines. My
colleague was bereft.

I thought about this family off and on during the day, and
even more as I drove home that night. I had a strong sense
I needed to offer what help I could, even on my entry-level
salary. I knew I could get a gift card for an inexpensive
major chain store where they could replace many basic

items. But the more I thought about this family in particular, about their school-age children, I kept thinking how all those special pieces of clothing had disappeared along with the towels and undershirts. Maybe the daughter had lost a dress that had been made by her grandmother. Maybe a special shirt in the latest fashion, now gone. Those are the hard things to justify replacing when you've just lost everything. I decided to give my friend a gift card from a store with some distinction, a place to perhaps purchase something beyond the basic necessities. I sealed it up in an interoffice envelope, without a card, and smiled. I prayed and hoped they would use it with great joy.

A few days later, at the beginning of a meeting, my colleague asked if he could speak. "I don't know which one of you sent the gift card, and I know you don't want me to know. But I want to thank you for such a great reminder that God is active and is taking care of my family. It meant so much to my wife to know she could take our children to such a nice store and let them pick out some things to replace what was taken."

My moment of service lasted only briefly, but I've never forgotten the profound lesson it taught me about serving people. It made me realize that while it is important to serve by sharing our resources with ministries and missions, it is another thing entirely to serve another individual. Jesus saw people with specific, personal needs. He addressed each need uniquely. Some were spoken to, such as the Samaritan woman at the well. Some were touched, such as the man with leprosy in Matthew 8:3. Some were not even seen and yet were healed, such as the servant of the centurion (Matthew 8:5–13). Everything is personal with God. Every creative, redemptive act of God is a result of seeing a particular need in a particular place at a particular time.

Why is this important? Because the Christ cannot achieve what he wants in your life if you solely serve others as anonymous entities. In "Seeing Faces behind the Needs" (*Everyday Matters Bible for Women*), Cindy Crosby writes that she started volunteering at a food pantry out of a "vague sort of guilt about world hunger." But after she met real people with real stories who had found themselves in need of food, whenever she thought of the hungry she "no longer saw headlines, but faces. And that has made all the difference."

In this study's Scripture passage, Jesus tells the story of the Good Samaritan. Samaritans and Jews did not get along. In fact, the Samaritans were despised by the Jews. When the Samaritan man saw the Jewish man who had been robbed and beaten half-dead, he overlooked the enmity between their people; instead he saw a human being who desperately needed help. He saw a face that was bloody and bruised, a body that was broken. Then he went over to the injured man and soothed his wounds. Not only that, but he spent money to take the stranger—the enemy—to an inn, where he stayed with him for another day. No doubt the Samaritan had somewhere else he'd planned to be by the next day. But he gave his time and inconvenienced himself in order to serve another in need, even paying in advance for further care for the patient. What a beautiful story of true service, and even of loving one's enemies.

> *"The first question which the priest and the Levite
> asked was: 'If I stop to help this man, what will
> happen to me?' But . . . the good Samaritan reversed
> the question: 'If I do not stop to help this man, what
> will happen to him?'"* —Martin Luther King Jr.

*As you study this chapter, consider your spiritual
gifts and how you can specifically offer these
gifts to the people struggling around you.*

1. In Luke 10:37, Jesus agrees that the Good Samaritan
showed mercy to the stranger. What do you think mercy
has to do with serving others?

2. In Luke 19, Jesus offers to share a meal with Zacchaeus,
another person despised by the Jews. How does Zacchaeus
respond? What does his response tell you about simple acts
of service?

3. Psalm 139:13–16 tells of the great care with which God has created us. How should your service to others reflect that knowledge?

4. Read Joshua 2. Why does Rahab help the Israelite spies? What happens as a result in Jericho, and to her and her family? Have there been times when you had to go against others because of your fear of the Lord?

5. Read John 13:13–15. What is the model Jesus is offering us of service?

6. In Jeremiah 22:3, the Lord says to the king of Judah, "Be fair-minded and just. Do what is right! Help those who have been robbed; rescue them from their oppressors. Quit your evil deeds! Do not mistreat foreigners, orphans, and widows. Stop murdering the innocent!" This call for justice and right behavior toward others is something we read often from the Old Testament prophets, which shows how critical doing right is to God. How can you serve others by acting on God's commands in this verse?

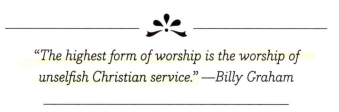

"The highest form of worship is the worship of unselfish Christian service." —Billy Graham

Points to Ponder

When we serve in personal ways, we say to others, *I see you.* At the same time, it can make you more attentive to the ways God sees *you.*

- What are ways you can serve others in personal ways?

- How can you be praying and preparing to help in this way?

Prayer

Lord Jesus, you came to us as a human to serve and save us in a particular time in history, in a particular place. Thank you for showing us how to serve others by using your example. Please give me a heart of service today and send me to a divine "service appointment."

Add your prayer in your own words.

Amen.

Put It into Practice

Find a way to serve others in personal ways this week, whether it's filling a need you know about at work, in your neighborhood or church, or with a local ministry.

Take-away Treasure

At the end of life we will not be judged by how many diplomas we have received, how much money we have made, how many great things we have done. We will be judged by "I was hungry and you gave me something to eat. I was naked and you clothed me. I was homeless, and you took me in."

—Mother Theresa

CHAPTER 2

The Shape of Humility

Serving in Silence

All of you, serve each other in humility, for

"God opposes the proud
but favors the humble."

So humble yourselves under the mighty power of
God, and at the right time he will lift you up in honor.

1 PETER 5:5-6

For this study, read Philippians 2:1–8.

A few days after Christmas, I called my mother. We had been together for the holidays, and she was still visiting my sister at her new home. When she began to describe the house to me, telling me how much I would love it, my heart sank. She had no memory of our five-day visit, of seeing her grandchildren, or any of us. Like so many events in the past year, this one was enjoyed for the moment—but then it was gone.

This turn of events has distressed me in some obvious ways, primarily concern for her health and well-being. But I've also realized this year that much of my alarm is about me.

Until her memory began to sputter, I counted on her re-membering our lives together—I wanted her to be able to remember all the service, all the acts of kindness she had re-ceived so she would know she was loved. And to be honest, I wanted not just the "thank you" of the moment—I wanted all the good times to be piled up in her memory so I could point them out to her and say, "Remember when we . . ." Without knowing it, I'd been conducting a transaction with my mother: *I will listen to every story as many times as you need to tell it. I can take hours for simple errands, as long as you will remember.*

But without her consent, time and age took away memo-ries of all sorts, leaving her children to grapple with the results. For me, that has included coming to terms with serving in humility. Serving Mom now means there will be no memory of our time—no shared experience, no lasting connection forged through our years together. It means taking care of the need of the moment and then moving on. It means that, at times, Mom will probably wonder why her daughters don't visit more often, why we don't call her. This is difficult for everyone to bear. We not only want to serve the woman who served us all our lives, but we also want her to know that we serve her. We want to "get points" for doing the right thing. And while it continues to be a hard adjust-ment, it also makes for daily acts of submission, daily sur-render of my will—and my ego.

The discipline of service gives a shape to humility, creating it within us. As Richard Foster says in "The Prescription for Pride: Service" (*Everyday Matters Bible for Women*), service provides training against pride and is much more effective than "trying" to be humble. Instead, service puts us into the actual practice of humility, taking us "through the many little deaths of going beyond ourselves."

Service to others fosters humility in another way, as well. Who could volunteer at a local shelter or hospital without realizing that "there but for the grace of God go I"? Anytime we help another, it should serve as a reminder that every blessing we have is a gift from God.

How do we serve with humility? We look to Christ as our example. We look at the many acts of service Christ performed on earth. The feeding (John 6:15). The healing (John 9:6–7). The foot washing (John 13:1–5). The compassion (Matthew 14:14). Though we call attention to these moments, there is no sense that Jesus himself saw them as remarkable moments. Serving others, with or without a crowd, was for Christ an expression, an outgrowth, of life with God.

Most acts of service are humbling by their very nature. We put other's needs before our own. We wait in a doctor's office with a friend. We stop by a hospital. We search store shelves for one brand in particular, because we know our friend prefers it. Sometimes the effort is acknowledged, sometimes not. And so the urge comes to take this moment, where the shape of humility is complete, and distort it by broadcasting our efforts to others. We explain why we are late: we were busy performing a selfless act; we drop our acts of service into conversations. We report on our deeds as we ask for prayer.

No one but you and God know your motives for telling others how you've served. But of this I am sure—more is gained by keeping silent. We learn how to retain that humble shape of a disciple by consistency and by silence. Then one day we will be as astonished as the righteous ones of Matthew 25:37, who could not think of when they had served the Lord, because it was just what they did each day.

"Humility is a byproduct of belief in the gospel of Christ." —Timothy Keller

As you study this chapter, consider the ways you currently serve others. How much recognition do you receive for your service?

1. In Philippians 2:7, Paul tells us that Christ gave up his divine privileges and "took up the humble position of a slave." As disciples, what can we learn about serving by considering ourselves in the humble position of a slave?

2. In Proverbs 29:23, Solomon writes that "humility brings honor." How does that happen in your life? Where does the honor come from?

3. Read Ruth 1–2. As a widow, she is already humble. She has little or no standing in her community. She goes further, though, into service and humility by accompanying her mother-in-law back to Israel, leaving all that is familiar. In moments when you've felt powerless, what is your response? Can you consider the actions—the faith and trust of Ruth—as offering another way to look at serving?

4. Proverbs 11:2 says, "Pride leads to disgrace, but with humility comes wisdom." Has there been a time in your life when you experienced the truth of this proverb?

5. We know that service is essential to God, and we know true greatness comes only to the humble. In Matthew 18:1–4, Christ points us in the direction of children as an example of the "great" in his kingdom. In term of humility, what qualities do children possess that you believe Christ is pointing us to adopt as believers?

6. In "Jesus-Style Service" (*Everyday Matters Bible for Women*), Kelli Trujillo states that the service of Jesus was often bottom-rung, no credit service. Think of the ways you serve others. Do they mirror Jesus in this way?

"The best way to find yourself is to lose yourself in the service of others." —Mahatma Gandhi

Points to Ponder

Tim Keller writes in "The Advent of Humility" (*Everyday Matters Bible for Women)* that "gracious, self-forgetful humility . . . is largely missing in the church."

- Consider your own local congregation. Has sanctimony crept into your acts of service?

Not all service is a discipline. Some service is the result of our spiritual gifts and comes as easy as breathing. As Dallas Willard writes in *The Spirit of the Disciplines: Understanding How God Changes Lives*, "Not every act that may be done as a discipline need be done as a discipline. I will often be able to serve another simply as an act of love and righteousness, without regard to how it may enhance my abilities to follow Christ. . . . But I may also serve another to train myself away from arrogance, possessiveness, envy, resentment, or covetousness."

- What are your spiritual gifts? How do you use them on a daily basis?

Prayer

Lord, you have given me a living example of humility through service. I ask you to instill in me a humble spirit as I go through my day. When I begin to feel smug or proud of my service, remind me that it is only through your grace that I'm able to serve. Help me to remember that "there, but for the grace of God, go I."

Add your prayer in your own words.

Amen.

Put It into Practice

Look at the content of your calendar for the week ahead. Identify places in your week where the needs of others are placed before your own. For each act, take a moment to focus your attention on Christ and ask him for the grace to perform each one in humility.

Take-away Treasure

Most of us would rather be in the position of having the resources to help another rather than to be the one in need. Every time we are asked to help, that is an opportunity for gratitude.

> The Simple Path
>
> *Silence is Prayer*
> *Prayer is Faith*
> *Faith is Love*
> *Love is Service*
> *The Fruit of Service is Peace*
>
> —Mother Teresa

CHAPTER 3

Stopping What Stops Us from Serving

Going beyond Ourselves

> So he got up from the table, took off his robe,
> wrapped a towel around his waist, and poured water
> into a basin. Then he began to wash the disciples'
> feet, drying them with the towel he had around him.

JOHN 13:4-5

For this study, read John 13:1–17.

Most of the time, whether I am serving or being served, what trips me up most of all are my own thoughts—and my pride. Two events this past Lenten season reminded me of my own failing in service. A good friend was trying to adjust to life after a surgical procedure that went badly, which left her unable to use her left arm and leg. She is also unable to drive. After months of support from her family and friends, she still needs rides to therapy appointments about four days a week. I love my friend, but I work full time, and I just didn't see how I could be of much help. But the Spirit kept up his work in me, prompting me to look again at my calendar. I *could* take her to her appointment once a week, because it coincided with my lunch hour. But still I was reluctant to offer. Why? I was afraid, and not of anything important. I was afraid my schedule would be upended. I was afraid she would need other rides to other places, and I'd have to decline, and I hate saying no. All this is the crazy internal talk I went through for a few days before finally calling and offering what I could.

The other event happened during our Lenten Bible study. On the day we were to discuss Jesus washing the feet of the disciples, our pastor walked into the room with a bucket and a towel, and my heart seized up. I couldn't believe how quickly my body reacted to the sight of that bucket and towel. *Is he really going to wash our feet? What will I do? What will I say? Am I going to have to wash the feet of some-one too?* In those moments of panicked self-examination, I realized I am just as uncomfortable being served as I am serving. My well-ordered life gets messy, and my self-sufficiency is exposed for the sham it is. I am really not good at this discipline of service. I love the idea of it—but the reality is something quite opposite.

Richard Foster likens this struggle with pride to "training" rather than "trying." In "The Prescription for Pride: Service" (*Everyday Matters Bible for Women*), he writes:

> It is important to distinguish 'training' from 'trying.' I might try *very hard* to win a marathon race, but if I have not trained, I will not even finish, not to mention win. On the day of the race, no amount of trying will make up for the failure to train. It is the training that will enable me to participate effectively in the race. The same is true in the spiritual life.

As we saw in the last chapter, Foster talks about "the many little deaths of going beyond ourselves." These "little deaths" occur when we set aside our own need and focus on the needs of others. It can be as simple as giving up a favorite television program, or something more drastic in your life. In these "little deaths," God transforms us and enables us to "see ourselves as part of a whole. The spiritual discipline of service can nurture in us a proper perspective toward others, ourselves, and God."

So maybe allowing someone to do something nice for you is in itself dying a "little death"—the death of pride in being vulnerable and appreciative of the love offered to you in Jesus' name. As we reach out to others, both for giving and receiving, we indeed find ourselves becoming an active and alive part of the body of Christ.

"The place God calls you to is the place where your deep gladness and the world's deep hunger meet." —Frederick Buechner, Wishful Thinking

As you reflect on this chapter, ask God to show you the places you stop yourself from serving others.

1. What stops you from offering to serve others?

2. What stops you from accepting the service of others?

3. For many women, accepting service from others is much harder than serving. Can you remember the last time you gratefully accepted service? What are some of the reasons you find yourself giving for not allowing others to serve you?

4. When people offer to serve your family, do you have the same reaction?

5. According to 1 Corinthians 12:7, why are we given spiritual gifts?

6. What are some "little deaths" you can die this week? How can you be more open to the needs of others and your own?

"When you sense God is tugging on your heart or convicting you, I encourage you to say yes to God. Don't hold back. Don't overthink it or analyze all the what-ifs—just jump in with your heart. From there, take time to get educated; listen to what others have to say, glean wisdom from others, and get training. Be the best servant you can be!" —Kay Warren

Points to Ponder

The discipline of service requires us to acknowledge two truths that will be present as we serve. First, service will take more time than you think you have, and more energy than you have available. Second, your schedule will continue to be full of demands from others as well as desires of your own. Yet we can be encouraged. As Margo Starbuck writes in the *Everyday Matters Bible for Women*, our faithful response to serve in spite of our busy schedules "springs from noticing what moves God's heart."

• Who do you know needs your immediate help?

• If you are in need of help yourself, who can you reach out to?

Prayer

God, my life is not my own. My schedule is not my own. They are yours, to be used for your glory. May my service be framed by these truths today.

Add your prayer in your own words.

Amen.

Put It into Practice

Dust off your someday list, your dreams of how you would serve God "if only . . ." How can you shape that dream to start on it today?

Take-away Treasure

It's possible what stops you at times is good—you are already serving well. And sometimes it stems from our fear, or selfish desires. Don't paint all your reasons for saying "no" to service with the same brush. This week, carefully reflect on what stops you for each opportunity.

Wherever you are, that is where the kingdom of God is at work. —Will and Lisa Samson, Justice in the Burbs

CHAPTER 4

True Religion

Serving Where Needed

"For I was hungry, and you fed me. I was thirsty,
and you gave me a drink. I was a stranger, and
you invited me into your home. I was naked, and
you gave me clothing. I was sick, and you cared
for me. I was in prison, and you visited me."

MATTHEW 25:35-36

For this study, read Matthew 25:31–46.

A friend of mine is a partner at a busy accounting firm. He
logs long hours with clients and loves his job. Recently, his
church asked him to consider becoming an elder—an honor
to be sure, but one that is taken seriously and comes with
a large time commitment. He and his wife also have three
children still in grade school. I knew he was struggling with
this opportunity—it was ministry, which he longed to do
more of, but it would require a lot of time.

After a few weeks, I asked how the decision process was
going, and he shared, with a look of complete contentment,
that he'd declined the invitation to join the elders at this

point. He shared with me the conversation that helped him decide.

> *I was discussing my dilemma with a mentor I meet with regularly, and he asked me how much time I usually spend when I'm with each of my clients. I thought about it and told him about forty-five minutes to an hour. Then he asked me how much time I needed to spend to get the business accomplished. I answered that the business part can be done in twenty to thirty minutes. He asked me why I spend twice as much time with my clients. The answer is that people's finances aren't just about their bank account and their taxes. This is also about their life and family, and they have worries and dreams. And most of the time they need to talk about all that, too. Then my mentor suggested to me that I am already in ministry. I'd never thought about it that way, but it really is, even if it doesn't carry the "ministry" title.*

As Kevin Miller says in "Serving behind the Scenes" (*Everyday Matters Bible for Women*), "It can be very hard to serve when our service goes unnoticed. But true service *is* often hidden." It certainly was for my friend. It was so embedded in his day that he didn't recognize it until someone else showed it to him. And within service provided anonymously are great gifts for us—we are free to stay humble and to stay focused on the One we really serve: the Lord Jesus. As he said to the disciples in the parable of the sheep and the goats in Matthew 25: "I tell you the truth, when you did it to one of the least of these my brothers and sisters, you were doing it to me!" (Matthew 25:40). In large part, our ability to actually *live* Christian lives, rather than wishing for them, is directly related to how we serve. As Keri Wyatt Kent writes in "Kingdom Service" (*Everyday Matters Bible for Women*),

By serving and ministering to the hungry, the sick, the pris-
oner; by extending hospitality to strangers and outcasts
(Matthew 25:35–36). This is what it is live in the kingdom
right now: to live in the way of Jesus, responding to his teach-
ings and example of love and service.

God has given each of you a gift from his
variety of spiritual gifts. Use them well to
serve one another. (1 Peter 4:10)

**As you study this chapter, think of the acts of
service hidden within your own daily routine as
well as acts of hidden service that you could add.**

1. James 1:27 says, "Pure and genuine religion in the sight
of God the Father means caring for orphans and widows
in their distress and refusing to let the world corrupt you."
When you read these words, how does it change your view
of service that pleases God?

2. Who are the "orphans and widows" around you? What can you do to serve them?

3. Micah 6:8 offers a clear look at what matters to God. How can you live out this verse?

4. In "Gifted for a Purpose" (*Everyday Matters Bible for Women*), Nancy Ortberg writes, "We develop and nurture our gifts as we use them—and we best use them in service to others as we seek to build the church." How are your gifts—whether in vocation or ministry or family life—used to serve others?

5. In Mark 1:40–45, Jesus does the unthinkable and touches a leper. Are there risky acts of service God is calling you to?

6. Like the accountant friend in this chapter, are there areas where you are really serving others when you didn't think you were? How can you look at your work—your daily life— as ministry?

"Look at God's incredible waste of His saints, according to the world's judgment. God seems to plant His saints in the most useless places. And then we say, 'God intends for me to be here because I am so useful to Him.' Yet Jesus never measured His life by how or where He was of the greatest use. God places His saints where they will bring the most glory to Him, and we are totally incapable of judging where that may be." —Oswald Chambers

Points to Ponder

Just because we serve people doesn't mean they will change who they are. Selfish people can stay selfish. Bitter people often remain bitter. As we consider our own motivations for change, we must resist the temptation to require a change of heart as the "price" of our service.

- What do you need to change in your life in order to serve more?

- Are there ministries at your church or a local organization to which you feel called? Is something keeping you from becoming involved? If so, what can you do to overcome it?

Prayer

Lead me today, Jesus, into the paths of service that will bring glory only to you.

Add your prayer in your own words.

Amen.

Put It into Practice

Sometimes our biggest obstacle in serving anonymously comes from those around us. Between friends who sing our praises and the ease of social media reporting, it's all too easy for others to generously commend our actions. This week, decide on who you can serve, and then tell no one your plans.

Take-away Treasure

Read Matthew 25:31–46 again. When you finish, close your eyes, and imagine yourself as one of those present with Christ. As you imagine him speaking to you, what is he saying? Are you among his sheep? Can you envision times when you offered water, food, or shelter to those in need?

Notes / Prayer Requests

_____

_____

_____

_____

_____

_____

_____

_____

_____

_____

_____

_____

_____

_____

_____

_____

_____

Notes / Prayer Requests

_____

_____

_____

_____

_____

_____

_____

_____

_____

_____

_____

_____

_____

_____

_____

_____

_____

Mentoring

CHAPTER 1

Being Teachable

Mentoring the Mentor

"Take my yoke upon you. Let me teach you,
because I am humble and gentle at heart, and
you will find rest for your souls. For my yoke is
easy to bear, and the burden I give you is light."

MATTHEW 11:29-30

For this study, read 1 Samuel 3 and John 1:35–50.

Despite my best efforts, I was struggling so much at work
that I began to feel hopeless. For many months, I'd been log-
ging long hours and sleeping fitfully, only to start the cycle
again the next day. I couldn't understand it. I had a master's
degree and had always excelled at my jobs. I didn't know
if my failures at work had led to hating my job, or if hating
my job had led to the failures. It all became a blur of defeat,
defensiveness, and despair. My mother, always my kindest
supporter, asked my uncle, who worked in human resources
consulting, to give me a call. In a conversation frequently
interrupted by my breaking into tears, he listened, asked
a few questions, and then gathered his thoughts. "I don't

suppose there's a way to leave the position any time soon?"
he asked. There wasn't. The job market was tight, and I
had lots of student loans and living expenses to pay. He
understood, and I was ready to listen and learn. What he
suggested countered all the negative talk I'd been feeding
myself. "You're too young to stop learning," he said. "Even in
a bad situation there are things you can learn. Make this job
your classroom."

Indeed, I was too young to stop learning. And so are you.
After talking with my uncle, light streamed into the dark
room I'd been inhabiting, and what had seemed impossible
became possible. Though I was an experienced professional,
I needed a wise guide, someone who knew the geography of
my situation and could help me navigate the thorny path I
was on.

Whether we are new believers or long-time followers of
Christ, we all need wise guides. As a mentor, it is easy to
forget that even mentors need guidance. Jesus routinely
asked those who were used to being in the lead—directing
their own path—to follow him. As you study the discipline
of mentoring, the first lesson is to be teachable—to see
yourself as teachable. Look to the Scriptures, and as you do,
examine your own heart. Pray for a humble spirit, ready to
receive. Ask the Lord for his special guidance, and then look
around you and find someone you know who might have
wisdom and experience they can share with you.

"You asked, do you have to be old before you are wise? No, I don't think so. But you do have to know how to listen." —Eugene Peterson, Wisdom, Silence, and Learning How to Die

As you study this chapter, think about your need for spiritual growth and who can help you.

1. In "Mentors Help Us Hear God's Voice" (*Everyday Matters Bible for Women*), Priscilla Shirer reminds us that we all need an Eli—someone who helps us hear God's voice, as Eli did for Samuel in 1 Samuel 3. Consider the people in your life. Who is your Eli? For whom could you act as an Eli?

2. How does the discipline of mentoring connect with the discipline of submission?

3. In "Becoming a Mentored Disciple" (*Everyday Matters Bible for Women*), Adele Ahlberg Calhoun reminds us we live in a culture that is "captivated by grandiosity" and our "deep need to appear larger than life." Contrast this with the small things Jesus points to in the parables: the lost sheep and lost coin in Luke 15, and the small mustard seed in Matthew 13. How does our preoccupation with living large hamper our spiritual growth as disciples?

4. When the Gospels record a question asked of Jesus, we often learn that people weren't seeking a real answer; they were only looking for confirmation of their own views (read Luke 10:29–37 about the parable of the Good Samaritan). There are others, however, who exhibit a teachable spirit. Look at John 3 and the story of Nicodemus. What does this passage offer you as a model of teach-ability?

5. In 1 Kings 19:19–21, we have the invitation of Elijah to Elisha to follow and learn from him. Take a look at the four parts: Elijah's invitation, Elisha's response, Elijah's rebuttal, and Elisha's actions. What can you learn from the passage about mentoring and being mentored?

6. If you are an Elijah, is there perhaps an Elisha God is calling you to mentor?

"There are no self-made people. We are all shaped by our relationships, for good or ill. Yet sometimes people treat their spiritual journey as a solo flight; they like the independence of listening to God on their own and charting their own course. This is not what the first Jesus-followers did; they kept company with Jesus as with one another." —Adele Ahlberg Calhoun, "Becoming a Mentored Disciple" (Everyday Matters Bible for Women)

Points to Ponder

You may, as a seasoned mature disciple, be used to taking on the role of a mentor. And maybe those around you just assume you've got it all together. But we all need mentors, people to help us stretch and grow. Even if you're a mentor, don't be afraid to ask for mentoring.

- Spend time with God, asking him for guidance on where you need to grow spiritually, and then write down the answers here.

- What are some steps you can take to become more vulnerable and open to listening to others? Search yourself out for hidden pride and where you may need to learn humility, remembering that there are indeed, as Adele Ahlberg Calhoun says, "no self-made people."

- She also says that "we are all shaped by our relationships, for good or ill." Are there people in your life who have a negative influence on you? Consider your relationship with these people and how it might be affecting you for "ill."

Prayer

Jesus, you are my best teacher in the life of faith. Today I submit my life to your teaching and ask you to provide wisdom as I guide, as well as wise guides for me. Help me to be humble and learn from others, and lead me to those who will help shape me into the godly woman you want me to be.

Add your prayer in your own words.

Amen.

Put It into Practice

You are on a journey as a disciple of Christ, but you are not alone. Your life is filled with fellow travelers who have direction to offer; in turn you will offer direction to others. Today, offer your willing heart to the Lord. Ask him to create within you an attitude of tender teach-ability. Be patient—and alert—as you wait for his answer.

Take-away Treasure

As you seek mentors, prayerfully ask God to reveal your needs to you. It may be that you need a mentor for a specific area of your life. Or you may need a mentor to help you see how all the disparate aspects of life shape each other. Be open to the possibility that your mentor may not be someone currently in your close circle of friends.

> *Receiving the mentoring from those more spiritually mature, in return providing mentorship to those who are growing— this is the cycle of spiritual growth God put into motion for his people. Who will you invest in? Who will you listen to?*
> —Kelli B. Trujillo, "Biblical Female Mentors" (Everyday Matters Bible for Women)

CHAPTER 2

Mentoring in Love

Being a "Spiritual Cairn"

You have heard me teach things that have been
confirmed by many reliable witnesses. Now
teach these truths to other trustworthy people
who will be able to pass them on to others.

2 TIMOTHY 2:2

For this study, read 2 Timothy 2 and 1 Corinthians 10:31–11:2.

Each year our church spends a month hosting a treasure hunt
for the children. But what makes this treasure hunt special is
that it isn't the seeking out of candy or toys—it's a hunt for
the older members of our congregation. Each week children
receive clues to help them find their treasure—notes that
reveal our personalities, the things we love, the ways God
has revealed himself to us. The idea has been to help children
(and adults) connect with those outside their age group, to
help children see adults as people with interesting life experi-
ences and faith journeys. And let's face it, we adults feel like
kids again, playing hide and seek!

Over the years, the treasure hunt has helped our small church become a place where we are known and where we know others. It's given us a way to gently light the paths of our smallest members, offering guidance through example and experience, and through personal affirmations.

We mentor best when our motivations are the love of Christ and love for his people. In "Stones That Speak" (*Everyday Matters Bible for Women*), Cindy Crosby suggests that we can become for each other "spiritual cairns." A cairn is a small pile of stones hikers leave for each other to show the correct path at critical junctures on a trail. Like those rocky cairns, we have the same ability to show others the way of discipleship.

But we can also have unhealthy motives for mentoring. As Mindy Caliguire writes in "Why We Mentor" (*Everyday Matters Bible for Women*), lacking love can lead to disastrous outcomes. She wisely suggests we become aware of several unhealthy motivators:

- We want to leave a legacy.

- We like being "the one" who is sought after in a community.

- We prefer meddling in other people's problems.

- We have a need to teach.

- We may be inclined toward codependency.

- We like the label of mentor.

As opportunities to mentor come your way, task yourself first and foremost with the commandment to love.

"*The delicate balance of mentoring someone is not creating them in your own image, but giving them the opportunity to create themselves.*" —*Steven Spielberg*

> **As you study this chapter, think of those you mentor. What is your motivation in your role?**

1. In Acts 11:19, we read of believers who shared the good news of Christ with the Gentiles. What was the outcome in verse 21? What was Barnabas's response in verse 23?

2. Ultimately, Barnabas sought out Saul and they both returned to Antioch. Read Acts 11:26–30. How long did Paul and Barnabas stay in Antioch? What does that suggest to you about the nature of mentoring in love?

3. As Mindy Caliguire mentioned, we can have unhealthy motives for not mentoring others. What stops you from mentoring others?

4. Read a brief section of the book of Proverbs. Which of the proverbs speak to you as a mentor?

5. Mindy Caliguire also says that many potential mentors put off mentoring because they feel inadequate—they don't know the Bible well enough, their own lives are barely together, or they just don't have enough time. Do you fall into any of these categories? If so, what can you do to overcome these self-imposed obstacles?

6. Is there anyone you feel you could come alongside and help in her life? If you are feeling a bit daunted about starting up a "mentoring" relationship, then just start with meeting this person for coffee or lunch.

And you yourself must be an example to them by
doing good works of every kind. (Titus 2:7)

Points to Ponder

In Matthew 5:14–16, Jesus tells his followers they are the light of the world. Most of the time we tend to read his words and think of "the world" as those outside the body of Christ. But believers also need light and guidance.

- Read through the passage in Matthew again, thinking of your local body as part of the world. What are some ways you can mentor in love, shining the light of Christ within the body?

It's gratifying when a mentoring relationship goes well— when the words we speak are taken in and we see the fruit of the Spirit bloom. When our prayers are answered and growth takes place. But often that is not the case. The work of God in the life of a believer takes its own pace, and God is not maturing them so *we* can feel good about our investment of time and energy.

- Is there someone who doesn't seem to "get it"? Before giving up on her, have you looked at her as you look at yourself? That is, recognizing that you and she are both flawed but devoted followers of Jesus?

Prayer

Lord, may I love those I serve, so that you may be served well. Please show me who those people may be and how I can come alongside them to help where I can.

Add your prayer in your own words.

Amen.

Put It into Practice

Mentors should be sought. Your job is not to seek a person to mentor but to be ready to mentor in love. Look at the lives you influence right now—co-workers, children, and friends, members of your small group. What are the ways you can love them well today?

Take-away Treasure

In John 21:15–17, Jesus asks Peter the same question three times: Do you love me? He then commands Peter to feed his sheep. If we love Jesus, we feed his sheep. Consider your mentoring in love as one of the ways you feed his sheep.

> *Love is something that every one of us, at every stage of life's journey, can extend to others around us. This is core to how the body of Christ matures and grows: one person, one relationship, at a time.—Mindy Caliguire, "Why We Mentor"* (Everyday Matters Bible for Women)

CHAPTER 3

Investing in Others

What Real Mentoring Looks Like

God knows how often I pray for you. Day and
night I bring you and your needs in prayer to God,
whom I serve with all my heart by spreading the
Good News about his Son. One of the things I
always pray for is the opportunity, God willing,
to come at last to see you. For I long to visit you
so I can bring you some spiritual gift that will
help you grow strong in the Lord. When we get
together, I want to encourage you in your faith,
but I also want to be encouraged by yours.

ROMANS 1:9-12

For this study, read Acts 18:24–19:7.

Though I rarely use the word *mentor*, I actually have many
in my life. These are the people I turn to for advice; but
even more so, they are the people I observe closely. How do
they live? How do they respond to struggles? How do they
submit their will to serve God? And while we don't have

"mentoring sessions," what is in our relationship is that we are in consistent contact.

When I was growing up, my sister was always a mentor for me. She's just enough older that I could watch her and learn from her, and when the time came for any new venture, I could rely on her guidance. The only decision I think we made together was our decision to follow Christ; we were baptized the same Sunday night as teenagers, and thus began our life of faith with a biological sister and a sister in Christ at our side.

As adults, we haven't lived in the same state for over thirty years; but about five years ago, we realized we really missed our regular talks about our faith life. Phone calls and visits were consumed with catching up on kids and jobs and other things, but by the time we wanted to talk about what God had been teaching us, or what we were reading, someone needed something and we had to hang up. So we began a weekly phone call where conversation is only about reading and faith and God. We call it our "Conversations about Conversations" because we've found that *Conversations Journal* (www.conversationsjournal.com) gives us a great jumping-off point to talk about our faith lives. We read an article and block out a lunch hour each week to talk about what we've learned, how the writing intersected with our lives, or what we didn't agree with. Without fail, our readings lead us to talk about our Scripture readings and what God has been teaching us in the process.

For me this has become such a rich part of my week that I fight hard to preserve it. I love our time together. I love what I learn from my sister, what I learn from the word and from these thoughtful Christian writers. Possibly the most important part of the experience is how it keeps me continually filtering my daily life through the lens of my faith, keeping God at the center of it all.

Chances are that you have mentors like this too—mentoring that is "a natural extension of a person's care and concern for another person," as Rachel Jay writes in "Unofficial Mentors" (*Everyday Matters Bible for Women*). These are the people the writer of Proverbs 13:20 had in mind when he wrote, "Walk with the wise and become wise; associate with fools and get in trouble."

Whether you are the mentor or the one being mentored, your relationship will be one of investment in the lives of others, consistently and lovingly. In "Signs of Fruitful Mentoring" (*Everyday Matters Bible for Women*), Fred Smith suggests that a good mentoring relationship will include trust and confidence, unvarnished truth, and character development—the latter made possible by the Holy Spirit. All are important to remember and strive for as you mentor others.

"*Spoon feeding in the long run teaches us nothing but the shape of the spoon.*" —*E. M. Forster*

As you study this chapter, think of the people you find yourself watching and modeling your life after. Are they the mentors you need? Ask God for guidance as you follow the examples of others, and as others follow you.

1. In Acts 18:24–28, we read of the mentorship of Priscilla with her husband Aquila. How did they guide Apollos, according to this passage? (You can also read about Priscilla in Romans 16:3 and 2 Timothy 4:19.)

2. In Titus 2:3–5, older women are given clear instruction on the need to teach younger women, to model godly lives for them, and train them. According to the passage, what are older women to do? What are younger women to do?

3. In "Biblical Female Mentors" (*Everyday Matters Bible for Women*), Kelli Trujillo asks two important questions: "Who will you invest in? Who will you listen to?" What is your answer?

4. In Joshua 23, Joshua begins his final words to the people of Israel. How does Joshua mentor Israel? What are some of the things he says in Joshua 23 that would help anyone being mentored?

5. First Timothy is a letter from a mentor (Paul) to the one he is mentoring (Timothy). What can you tell about their mentoring relationship by reading this letter?

6. How does mentoring others fulfill Jesus' commandment in Matthew 22:37–39 to love our neighbors as ourselves?

"The mediocre teacher tells. The good teacher explains. The superior teacher demonstrates. The great teacher inspires." —William Arthur Ward

Points to Ponder

Fred Smith says that mentorship relationships should always be initiated, and maintained, by the person seeking a mentor—the "mentoree." In "Signs of Fruitful Mentoring," he writes, "The mentoree controls the continuation of the relationship. Sometimes a mentoring relationship becomes non-productive and should end. I accept this as normal."

- As you mentor, be aware it might only be for a season. Gracefully allow the relationship to end if needed.

- As the person being mentored, don't be afraid to bring a relationship to its graceful end.

Prayer

God, thank you for the gift of our relationships with others. Thank you for the direction of the Spirit. As I grow and share with others, may I seek always to please you.

Add your prayer in your own words.

Amen.

Put It into Practice

Take a moment to write down those who are your mentors, whether they know it or not.

- What do you learn from them?

- What would you like to learn from them?

- Now consider how much regular contact you have with those people. What can you rearrange in your schedule to make sure you have consistent interaction with them?

Take-away Treasure

The Bible gives us many examples of female mentorships to draw on as we seek to honor God in our mentoring relationships. Take some time to read through the book of Ruth and consider how Ruth and Naomi invested in each other's lives. Also read Luke 1 about Mary and Elizabeth, and about other women in the early church such as Priscilla (Acts 18:26) and Phoebe (Romans 16:1–2). May we all follow their lead in leading others along the Christian walk of faith.

> *Priscilla is a model of the power of disciple making: she exercised her gift of leadership and used it to pass on the truth of Christ to other men and women. She saw potential in leaders like Apollos and invested heavily in them. . . . Scripture paints a picture of her as someone who not only led by example but also got involved in others' lives—who walked alongside her brothers and sisters, helping them grow as Jesus' disciples.*
> —Nicole Unice, *"Priscilla: Invested in Others"* (Everyday Matters Bible for Women)

CHAPTER 4

"Imitate Me"

Following Paul as He Follows Christ

> So whether you eat or drink, or whatever you
> do, do it all for the glory of God. Don't give
> offense to Jews or Gentiles or the church of God.
> I, too, try to please everyone in everything I do.
> I don't just do what is best for me; I do what is
> best for others so that many may be saved.
>
> 1 CORINTHIANS 10:31-33

For this study, read Ephesians 4:1–16.

When I was teaching my children how to swim, the most
effective way was to have them watch me from the side of
the pool, then get in and do what I did. Over the course of a
summer, we went through these two simple steps again and
again. After eight weeks of watching and mimicking what
I did, the various disciplines of swimming—staying afloat,
achieving forward motion, and using a recognizable stroke
pattern—it all came together and the children were happily

swimming. What was daunting to them two months earlier had now become second nature.

Watch, imitate, repeat. It's one of the best methods to move someone from knowing about a skill to actually being skilled, and is a pattern used by mentors everywhere. In the Apostle Paul, God gave all of us a mentor to help us grow as disciples. Paul was passionate about mentoring. His letters and his travels were meant to share the gospel, but they were also to instruct, correct, and exhort believers, keeping them focused on Christ. His goal was spiritual maturity, yet he also realized that it was God who would do the work. As Roberta Hestenes says in "Mentoring toward Maturity" (*Everyday Matters Bible for Women*):

> But while our mentors can help someone become more mature, ultimately, it's not in our control. For example, Paul wrote letters, prayed, straightened out misunderstandings, and tried to reconcile relationships. However, Paul never said, "I am making you mature." Rather, he said Christ needs to be "fully developed" in our lives. . . . That's the Holy Spirit's work; as mentors, we seek to be colaborers with God.

In 1 Corinthians 11:1, Paul makes it clear to the church at Corinth that they "should imitate me, just as I imitate Christ." And he offers the same to us. On almost any subject we struggle with, we can look to the life and letters of Paul and find guidance and direction. We are reminded of the command to love, of the need for prayer and confession, and of the importance of living at peace with one another. We know enough about his life to know Paul understands disappointment, fear, and struggle, as well as success. He is a mentor who can sympathize, and yet he remains adamant about our need to pursue Christ and "strip off every weight that slows us down" (Hebrews 12:1). He does so, according to 1 Corinthians, "so that many may be saved."

In that way, our own successful mentorship also grows the kingdom of God. As you study the life and letters of Paul, look at the ways God has provided Paul as a mentor to you, offering you a model of faith to follow, so that in turn others may follow you.

"Like the Philippian Christians and all other Christians we read about in the New Testament, we need mature Christian models to pattern our lives after. . . . The Apostle Paul wins hands down. He doesn't just live the life of a Christian, he shares his Christian life with us as an example and model for us to follow. And, not only that, Paul boldly and clearly commands us to follow his example." —Greg Nance

As you study this chapter, consider what you know of the life of Paul. Set aside time to read about his conversion and ministry in the book of Acts. Imagine yourself with him, imitating his life as he pursues Christ.

1. In Romans 12:2, Paul writes, "Don't copy the behavior and customs of this world, but let God transform you into a new person by changing the way you think. Then you will learn to know God's will for you, which is good and pleasing and perfect." How can imitating Paul, or another mentor, help God transform you?

2. Read through Ephesians 4:7–16. If you are being mentored, do you see those qualities listed as the goal of your spiritual direction?

3. Read 2 Corinthians 1:3–4. What is the reason we are given comfort by God?

4. How do you see the discipline of mentoring and the discipline of outreach as complementary?

5. In "We Need Each Other" (*Everyday Matters Bible for Women*), Jeannette Bakke suggests that a mentor "can help us notice grace in ways we might have missed." Think about your role as a mentor. How can you help another believer notice grace?

6. Jeannette Bakke also suggests that we freely share with our mentor what we are learning from God in our quiet times and prayer. She says we need to say to ourselves, "I'm an ordinary person, but I have an extraordinary God, and it's okay to be just who I am, to ask God to be a part of the conversation, and to talk to another person about that." Do you feel spiritually inferior to your mentor or afraid to share? Or do you feel that these quiet times are private moments between you and God?

> *"Spiritual maturity is an ongoing journey, in*
> *which we continually press toward the mark . . . ;*
> *immaturity is complacency and self-satisfaction."*
> —*Roberta Hestenes, "Mentoring Toward Maturity"*
> (Everyday Matters Bible for Women)

Points to Ponder

In "We Need Each Other," Jeannette Bakke writes that "spiritual direction is grounded within Christian community." As you look at Paul as a spiritual director, remember his words were not given to individuals for their personal growth alone. We live as Christ followers within a faith community. As you mentor, keep these points in mind:

- Being a mentor can sometimes seem overwhelming, and actually isolating. You might be told things in confidence; you might be uncomfortable with some of the struggles shared.

- Consider the ways Paul approached his ministry, which almost always was done in partnership with another believer. Perhaps, in order to really allow for growth, your mentoring relationship should not be isolated to just one mentor and one person being mentored.

Prayer

God, you are the Author and Finisher of our faith. As I follow you, help me to be thankful for the life of Paul as he guides and corrects me. In the same way, help me also be a "Paul" for others.

Add your prayer in your own words.

Amen.

Put It into Practice

If someone was to imitate you as you imitated Christ, what would they be doing? Take a look this week at your actions. If someone imitated them, would God be glorified?

Take-away Treasure

Pick one of Paul's letters, using a Bible with a good introduction to each book. In the introduction, read about the context of Paul's letter—who was he writing to? What prompted the letter? Now consider your own life—what are similar motivations or situations you've faced? Write them down and then open Paul's letter as if were addressed to you or your church. Read it slowly, taking in his correction or encouragement as needed. Enjoy time with a great mentor!

Notes / Prayer Requests

_____

_____

_____

_____

_____

_____

_____

_____

_____

_____

_____

_____

_____

_____

_____

_____

_____

_____

Notes / Prayer Requests

_____

_____

_____

_____

_____

_____

_____

_____

_____

_____

_____

_____

_____

_____

_____

_____

_____

_____

_____

Leader's Guide

to Service & Mentoring

Thoughts on Where to Meet

- If you have the chance, encourage each group member to host a gathering. But make sure your host knows that you don't expect fresh baked scones from scratch or white-glove-test-worthy surroundings. Set the tone for a relaxed and open atmosphere with a warm welcome wherever you can meet. The host can provide the space and the guests can provide the goodies.

- If you can't meet in homes, consider taking at least one of your meetings on the road. Can you meet at a local place where people from your community gather? A park or a coffee shop or other public space perhaps.

- If you meet in a church space, consider partnering with another local church group and take turns hosting. How can you extend your welcome outside your group?

Thoughts on Ways to Foster Welcome

- If many of your members have a hard time meeting due to circumstances, look for ways to work around it. Consider providing childcare if there are moms who have difficulty attending, or meet in an accessible space if someone who might want to join has a disability. Does a morning time work better? Could you meet as smaller groups and then get together as a larger group for an event? Be flexible and see how you can accommodate the needs of the group. Incorporate "get to know you" activities to promote sharing. Don't take yourselves too seriously—let your humor shine through.

Incorporating Other Practices

- Lift your voices. Integrate worship throughout the study. Find songs that speak of service and mentoring.

- Commit to lift each other up in prayer. You may want to have a prayer walk as part of seeing opportunities to serve in your community, or prayer partners who might be able to meet at other times.

- Dig deep into the word. Take the study at your own pace but consider including passages for participants to read in between meetings. The *Everyday Matters Bible for Women* has a wealth of additional resources.

- Celebrate! Bring cupcakes and candles, balloons or anything celebratory to distribute to each member of the group. Ask each person to share something that they want to celebrate today, be it an event, a new insight, or anything they choose.

Service & Mentoring

The disciplines of service and mentoring will likely be lively and varied. Leading a group to discuss them will probably surprise you in how it brings out discussion among different members. Here are a few suggestions as you lead:

- Resist the temptation to spend time on "how to." Because both these disciplines can easily become a "checklist faith," plan your time together to be rich in the reading of Scripture and the focus on motivations. Keep any detail-oriented questions open ended, with the possibility of many "right" answers.

- Pray before you meet, and then also as a group, for a discussion free of judgment. We easily fall into the comparison trap when it comes to how we value different acts of service, and how many mentor relationships we've established. We must remember that our Adversary would like nothing better than to pull us apart, for us to stop meeting together to encourage one another. Your goal is growth of disciples. With God's help, create an atmosphere of no judgment, but also one that challenges each member to pursue righteousness with her whole heart.

- Challenge your group to be active on both the learning and the teaching side of these disciplines. Yes,

God wants us to serve and mentor. But he also wants us to be served and mentored.

- Listen to the needs of the group. It could be your group will become interested in a collective service project to put action with their studies. Be open to the working of the Spirit to use your group to seek God's favor, or to grow God's kingdom together.

- Add other spiritual disciplines to your discussions. As you study service, consider also the disciplines of outreach, hospitality, and submission. For your time together on the discipline of mentoring, you might want to bring in further disciplines of faith, confession, and community.

Follow-Up

Each of us is on a journey of discipleship. We will all attempt things that fail, or stumble our way through our service to God. As your group finishes your time together, make sure to stay in touch and encourage one another.

Additional Resources

- *Spiritual Mentoring: A Guide for Giving and Seeking Direction* by Keith R. Anderson and Randy D. Reese

- *The Friendships of Women* by Dee Brestin

- *Love Does* by Bob Goff

- *Spiritual Direction: Wisdom for the Long Walk of Faith* by Henri Nouwen

- *Say Yes to God* by Kay Warren

- *10 Power Principles for Christian Service* by Warren Wiersbe

- www.wearethatfamily.com

EVERYDAY MATTERS BIBLE STUDIES
for women

Spiritual practices for everyday life

Acceptance
Bible Study & Meditation
Celebration
Community
Confession
Contemplation
Faith
Fasting
Forgiveness
Gratitude
Hospitality
Justice

Mentoring
Outreach
Prayer
Reconciliation
Sabbath Rest
Service
Silence
Simplicity
Solitude
Stewardship
Submission
Worship

HENDRICKSON
PUBLISHERS

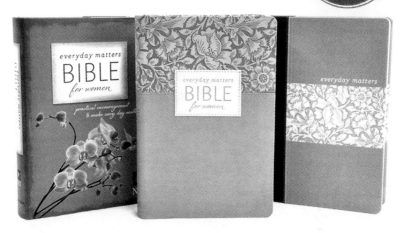